S0-AFK-231

ULTIMATE SUPERCARS

FERRARI 488 GTB

By Whitney Sanderson

WITHDRAWN

WORLD BOOK

BIGFOOT BOOKS

The Quest for Discovery Never Ends

This edition is co-published by agreement between Kaleidoscope and World Book, Inc.

Kaleidoscope Publishing, Inc.
6012 Blue Circle Drive
Minnetonka, MN 55343 U.S.A.

World Book, Inc.
180 North LaSalle St., Suite 900
Chicago IL 60601 U.S.A.

All rights reserved. No part of this book may be reproduced in any form without written permission from the publishers.

Kaleidoscope ISBNs
978-1-64519-028-8 (library bound)
978-1-64494-235-2 (paperback)
978-1-64519-128-5 (ebook)

World Book ISBN
978-0-7166-4329-6 (library bound)

Library of Congress Control Number
2019940226

Text copyright ©2020 by Kaleidoscope Publishing, Inc. All-Star Sports, Bigfoot Books, and associated logos are trademarks and/or registered trademarks of Kaleidoscope Publishing, Inc.

Printed in the United States of America.

FIND ME IF YOU CAN!

Bigfoot lurks within one of the images in this book. It's up to you to find him!

TABLE OF
CONTENTS

CHAPTER 1

MOVIE STAR

A red car whips around a turn. It's on a mountain road in Italy. Its wheels glint near the guard rail. The ground drops away on the other side.

The driver keeps his eyes on the road. He was trained to control this car. Someone who wasn't used to its speed could crash.

A black SUV follows. It has a camera. It can only film when the red car slows down. It can't go as fast. A **drone** films from above. The film crew lines the side of the road.

Ferrari is one of the most famous car brands in the world.

PARTS OF A
488 GTB

air intake slits

rear spoiler

engine in back

brake calipers

It's a big day for the Ferrari company. The film crew is making an advertisement. The ad is for its new sports car. The new car is the Ferrari 488 GTB. The video will go on Ferrari's website. Anyone across the world can watch it. But will it be exciting enough? Will people buy the car? The 488 GTB isn't cheap. And buyers who can afford one might buy other **luxury** cars.

Ferrari logo

The 488 GTB was released in 2015.

The video is shot and edited. The employees at Ferrari gather to watch it. Dramatic music begins to play. First, the red car zooms along a highway. Then it zigzags through the mountains. A moment later, it's speeding down a race track. Its engine roars.

FUN FACT
The Ferrari factory makes 8,400 cars a year.

A map is on the screen. It has words to describe the new car. It says "Desire," "Passion," and "Thrill." The last is "Driving Emotion." Then the video ends. There is a moment of silence. The employees start clapping. It's the perfect introduction to Ferrari's newest supercar.

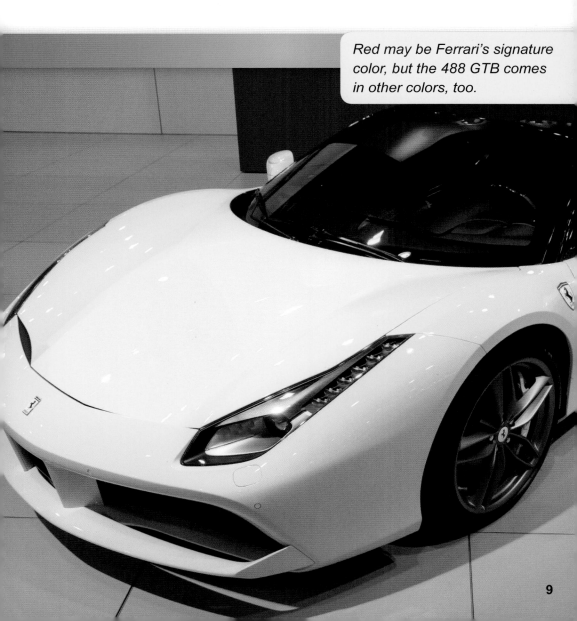

Red may be Ferrari's signature color, but the 488 GTB comes in other colors, too.

CHAPTER 2

ENZO'S LEGACY

Ten-year-old Enzo Ferrari cheered. The race cars roared down the road. It was a famous race in Italy.

The cars passed in a blur. They were almost close enough to touch. It was 1908. Most car races took place on the open road. There were no guard rails. Nothing separated the audience and the cars. Crashes were common.

Enzo didn't mind the danger. He dreamed of becoming a driver himself. But then World War I (1914–1918) started. He had to take a job in the army. His job was shoeing mules. Then the war ended. He eventually found a job with an Italian carmaker. It was Alfa Romeo. He began driving its cars in races. He became one of the top drivers.

THE PRANCING HORSE

Enzo Ferrari won a race in 1923. Afterward, he met the parents of a World War I pilot. The pilot's name was Francesco Baracca. Baracca's parents told Ferrari a special story. Baracca used to paint a prancing stallion on his airplanes. They suggested that using this symbol would bring Ferrari luck. Today, the black horse rears up against a yellow shield on all Ferrari cars.

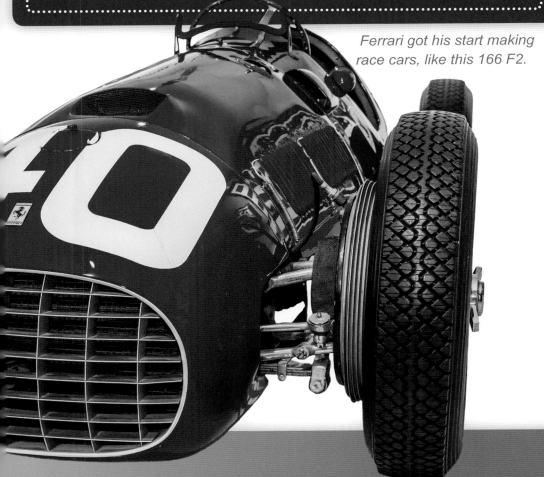

Ferrari got his start making race cars, like this 166 F2.

Ferrari started to **manufacture** his own cars in 1947. He died in 1988. By then, he was a legend. Ferrari was one of the most famous car companies in the world. Today, Ferrari makes both race cars and **road cars**. Its road cars are inspired by the race cars.

It was March 2015. A new Ferrari amazed a crowd. It was at the Geneva International Motor Show. This show happens every year in Switzerland. The car was called the 488 GTB.

Enzo Ferrari was born in Modena. There is a museum in his father's warehouse there. The factory in Maranello also has a museum.

Where the 488 GTB Is Made

Germany

Czechia

Austria

France

2·1

Italy

Mediterranean Sea

N
W◄┈┊┈►E
S

1 **Maranello, Italy:** Ferrari headquarters; the Ferrari factory, where the 488 GTB is assembled

2 **Modena, Italy:** The Scaglietti factory, where the doors are built

GTB stands for Gran Turismo Berlinetta. *Gran Turismo* is a car made for speed and style. *Berlinetta* is a car with a closed roof. Ferrari also released the 488 Spider. The Spider had an open roof.

FUN FACT
Ferrari drivers have won more than 5,000 races!

The 488 GTB replaced the 458 Italia. Both were inspired by the 308 GTB. It was from 1975. The 488 GTB is a two-seater sports car. Everything about it was designed to make jaws drop.

When the company started, Ferrari race cars had to be red. That was the color assigned to all Italian race cars.

CHAPTER 3

PEAK PERFORMANCE

Simona walks into a Ferrari dealership. She looks at a new 488 GTB. It is bright red. It looks fast.

Simona wants to buy a new car. She finds a salesperson. "What makes this car so special?"

"First of all, it's very fast," he answers. "Its top speed is 205 miles per hour (330 km/h). It can **accelerate** from 0 to 62 miles per hour (100 km/h) in 3 seconds."

Simona is impressed. She notices that the car has slits on the sides. They are near the rear wheels.

FUN FACT

The 488 GTB's top speed is three times as fast as a cheetah.

The 488 GTB was a hit at the Geneva Motor Show.

THE 488 GTB

Height: 4 feet (1.2 m)

Width: 6.4 feet (2 m)

COST: $292,182–$325,000

Length: 15 feet (4.6 m)

Weight: 3,252 pounds (1,475 kg)

Top Speed: 205 miles per hour (330 km/h)

Time from 0–62 miles per hour (0–100 km/h): 3 seconds

"Those are for air intake," the salesperson says. "The air helps power the engine. The car has a turbocharged **V8** engine. A turbocharger recycles gas fumes from the engine. This gives the car more power."

The salesperson opens the car door. Simona sits on the smooth leather seat. She grips the steering wheel.

"The body is made from aluminum," the salesperson says. "Many other cars use steel. But aluminum is lighter. This helps the car go faster."

Simona is starting to want the car. "How powerful is it?" she asks.

"Hold your horses!" he says. "The 488 GTB has 661 **horsepower.** That is more than earlier models. The 488 GTB has something called a blown rear spoiler. It's a hole on the back of the car. Air flows through it. That generates more **downforce**. It makes the car more stable."

Many of the car's controls are on the steering wheel.

"Does the car have any safety features?" Simona asks.

"Yes," he says. "One is side-slip angle control software. This helps stop the car from spinning out of control. That can happen if the driver turns too fast."

Simona looks at the Ferrari logo. It's on the steering wheel. She likes the car a lot. But it's very expensive.

The salesperson can tell she can't decide.

"This car has track-level performance," he says. "Driving this car is an experience. Its owner can feel the excitement of a race. Can you imagine feeling like Enzo Ferrari?"

"Can I take it for a test drive?" Simona asks.

"Of course." The salesperson smiles. Once a customer drives this car, it's as good as sold.

The display colors of the 488 GTB can be customized.

CHAPTER 4

FUN FACT

A fully customized Ferrari can take up to 2 years to be delivered.

Ferrari owners can fully customize their 488 GTBs, including choosing the colors of everything from the paint to the floor mats.

A FERRARI FUTURE

Bradley visits the Ferrari website. He can create his dream car. There are twenty-six colors to choose from. The most popular is *rosso corsa*. That means racing red. Bradley picks this one. He chooses the color of the wheels. He chooses their shape. He also customizes the **calipers**. He makes them *rosso corsa*, too.

Now for the inside. Bradley chooses the color of the seats. He also picks the material. They can be leather or carbon fiber. Carbon fiber seats are used in Ferrari race cars. Bradley can also change the **revcounter**. He sees his car at the end. Bradley is amazed. He can spin the car. He sees it from every angle. He imagines driving his Ferrari. The site gives him a code. He can take it to the dealership. They can get this car for him.

People use words like "speed" and "luxury" to define Ferrari. Ferrari's designer Flavio Manzoni has his own vision. He said, "A Ferrari must be sculpture in motion, a work of art."

The 488 GTB is no exception. It's won a dozen awards. One was the Autocar Awards Britain's Best Drivers' Car. Another was Auto Bild's Golden Steering Wheel Award. The British car magazine *Top Gear* also liked it. It named the 488 GTB 2016 Supercar of the Year.

Ferrari World in Abu Dhabi, United Arab Emirates

There's a Ferrari theme park called Ferrari World in Abu Dhabi. It has the world's fastest roller coaster, Formula Rossa.

FUN FACT
45 percent of Ferraris sold are red.

The Ferrari line hasn't ended with the 488 GTB. Ferrari has made several new road cars. The GTC4Lusso came out in 2017. The 812 Superfast did, too. The Portofino was released in 2018. So was another 488 model, the Pista.

Ferrari makes more than just cars. Fans can buy clothes, watches, toys, and more in Ferrari stores.

But the 488 GTB is not likely to go out of style. Two new Ferrari race cars are based on its design. They are the GTE and GT3. The judges of the 2016 Top Gear Award loved the car. They said, "This is Ferrari absolutely on its game. It's what supercars are about."

BEYOND

THE BOOK

After reading the book, it's time to think about what you learned. Try the following exercises to jumpstart your ideas.

THINK

THAT'S NEWS TO ME. The Ferrari 488 GTB was introduced to the public at the Geneva International Motor Show on March 3, 2015. How might news sources be able to fill in more detail about this? What new information could you find in news articles? Where could you go to find these sources?

CREATE

SHARPEN YOUR RESEARCH SKILLS. The Ferrari 488 GTB's engine is powered by a turbocharger. Where could you go in the library to find more information about turbocharged engines? Who could you talk to who might know more? Create a research plan. Write a paragraph about your next steps.

SHARE

WHAT'S YOUR OPINION? In Chapter Four, Ferrari's designer Flavio Manzoni says a Ferrari must be a work of art. Do you agree with Manzoni's opinion? Use evidence from the text to support your answer. Share your position and evidence with a friend. Does your friend agree with you?

GROW

DRAWING CONNECTIONS. Create a drawing that shows the connection between the Ferrari 488 GTB and car speed. What about the 488 GTB helps it go faster? How does learning about car speed help you better understand the 488 GTB?

RESEARCH NINJA

Visit *www.ninjaresearcher.com/0288* to learn how to take your research skills and book report writing to the next level!

RESEARCH

DIGITAL LITERACY TOOLS

SEARCH LIKE A PRO
Learn about how to use search engines to find useful websites.

FACT OR FAKE?
Discover how you can tell a trusted website from an untrustworthy resource.

TEXT DETECTIVE
Explore how to zero in on the information you need most.

SHOW YOUR WORK
Research responsibly— learn how to cite sources.

WRITE

GET TO THE POINT
Learn how to express your main ideas.

PLAN OF ATTACK
Learn prewriting exercises and create an outline.

DOWNLOADABLE REPORT FORMS

FURTHER RESOURCES

BOOKS

Cruz, Calvin. *Ferrari 458 Italia*. Bellwether Media, 2016.

James, Brant. *Formula One Racing*. Abdo Publishing, 2015.

Kingston, Seth. *The History of Ferraris*. PowerKids Press, 2019.

WEBSITES

Factsurfer.com gives you a safe,
fun way to find more information.

1. Go to www.factsurfer.com.

2. Enter "Ferrari 488 GTB" into the search box and click 🔍 .

3. Select your book cover to see a list of related websites.

GLOSSARY

accelerate: To accelerate means to increase in speed. The Ferrari 488 GTB can accelerate very quickly.

calipers: Calipers are a part of the brake system that slows the car's wheels. Buyers can customize the color of the calipers on their Ferrari.

downforce: Downforce is the force of air pushing down on a car because of a wing or other part. The wing on a supercar produces downforce to make the car easier to handle at high speed.

drone: A drone is a remote-controlled aircraft. Ferrari used a drone to film the car for its advertisement.

horsepower: One horsepower is the power it takes to lift 550 pounds one foot in one second. The 488 GTB has 661 horsepower.

luxury: Something that is a luxury is expensive and nice to have. Luxury cars are comfortable and high-tech.

manufacture: To manufacture means to make. Enzo Ferrari began manufacturing cars in 1947.

revcounter: The revcounter is an instrument that measures the speed of a car engine's rotation. Ferrari buyers can choose the color of the revcounter.

road car: A road car is a type of car that is legal to drive on a public street. The 488 GTB is a road car.

V8: A V8 engine is powered by eight cylinders. The 488 GTB has a V8 engine.

INDEX

PHOTO CREDITS

The images in this book are reproduced through the courtesy of: yousang/Shutterstock Images, font cover (car), pp. 3, 8; Maciej Bledowski/Shutterstock Images, front cover (road); Nadezda Murmakova/Shutterstock Images, pp. 4–5, 18; i viewfinder/Shutterstock Images, p. 5; Dong liu/Shutterstock Images, pp. 6, 6–7, 16–17, 30; Gautier22/Shutterstock Images, p. 7; VanderWolf Images/Shutterstock Images, p. 9; AP Images, p. 10; John_Silver/Shutterstock Images, pp. 10–11; Nico_Campo/iStockphoto, p. 12; Red Line Editorial, p. 13; Dan74/Shutterstock Images, pp. 14–15; Sjo/iStockphoto, p. 19; zavatskiy/iStockphoto, pp. 20–21; Cineberg/Shutterstock Images, pp. 22–23; Burachet/Shutterstock Images, p. 24; Kritsana Laroque/Shutterstock Images, pp. 24–25; Luca Santilli/Shutterstock Images, pp. 26–27; Everything You Need/Shutterstock Images, p. 27.

ABOUT THE AUTHOR

Whitney Sanderson is a writer from western Massachusetts. She is the author of numerous books for young readers, including five in the historical fiction series Horse Diaries and two in the history series Events That Changed America.